CAROL ANN DUFFY

Rapture

PICADOR

First published 2005 by Picador
an imprint of Pan Macmillan Ltd
Pan Macmillan, 20 New Wharf Road, London N1 9RR
Basingstoke and Oxford
Associated companies throughout the world
www.panmacmillan.com

ISBN 0 330 41280 9

1 3 5 7 9 8 6 4 2

A CIP catalogue record for this book is available from
the British Library.

Typeset by Macmillan Design Department
Printed and bound in Great Britain by
Mackays of Chatham plc, Chatham, Kent

Contents

Now no discourse, except it be of Love;
Now I can break my fast, dine, sup, and sleep
Upon the very naked name of Love.

Shakespeare, *Two Gentlemen of Verona* (II, iv, 137–9)

You

Uninvited, the thought of you stayed too late in my head,
so I went to bed, dreaming you hard, hard, woke with your name,
like tears, soft, salt, on my lips, the sound of its bright syllables
like a charm, like a spell.

                    Falling in love
is glamorous hell; the crouched, parched heart
like a tiger ready to kill; a flame's fierce licks under the skin.
Into my life, larger than life, beautiful, you strolled in.

I hid in my ordinary days, in the long grass of routine,
in my camouflage rooms. You sprawled in my gaze,
staring back from anyone's face, from the shape of a cloud,
from the pining, earth-struck moon which gapes at me

as I open the bedroom door. The curtains stir. There you are
on the bed, like a gift, like a touchable dream.

Text

I tend the mobile now
like an injured bird.

We text, text, text
our significant words.

I re-read your first,
your second, your third,

look for your small *xx*,
feeling absurd.

The codes we send
arrive with a broken chord.

I try to picture your hands,
their image is blurred.

Nothing my thumbs press
will ever be heard.

Name

When did your name
change from a proper noun
to a charm?

Its three vowels
like jewels
on the thread of my breath.

Its consonants
brushing my mouth
like a kiss.

I love your name.
I say it again and again
in this summer rain.

I see it,
discreet in the alphabet,
like a wish.

I pray it
into the night
till its letters are light.

I hear your name
rhyming, rhyming,
rhyming with everything.

Forest

There were flowers at the edge of the forest, cupping
the last of the light in their upturned petals. I followed you in,
under the sighing, restless trees and my whole life vanished.

The moon tossed down its shimmering cloth. We undressed,
then dressed again in the gowns of the moon. We knelt in the leaves,
kissed, kissed; new words rustled nearby and we swooned.

Didn't we? And didn't I see you rise again and go deeper
into the woods and follow you still, till even my childhood shrank
to a glow-worm of light where those flowers darkened and closed.

Thorns on my breasts, rain in my mouth, loam on my bare feet, rough
bark grazing my back, I moaned for them all. You stood, waist deep,
in a stream, pulling me in, so I swam. You were the water, the wind

in the branches wringing their hands, the heavy, wet perfume of soil.
I am there now, lost in the forest, dwarfed by the giant trees. Find me.

River

Down by the river, under the trees, love waits for me
to walk from the journeying years of my time and arrive.
I part the leaves and they toss me a blessing of rain.

The river stirs and turns, consoling and fondling itself
with watery hands, its clear limbs parting and closing.
Grey as a secret, the heron bows its head on the bank.

I drop my past on the grass and open my arms, which ache
as though they held up this heavy sky, or had pressed
against window glass all night as my eyes sieved the stars;

open my mouth, wordless at last meeting love at last, dry
from travelling so long, shy of a prayer. You step from the shade,
and I feel love come to my arms and cover my mouth, feel

my soul swoop and ease itself into my skin, like a bird
threading a river. Then I can look love full in the face, see
who you are I have come this far to find, the love of my life.

Haworth

I'm here now where you were.
The summer grass under my palms is your hair.
Your taste is the living air.

I lie on my back. Two juggling butterflies are your smile.
The heathery breath of the moor's simply your smell.
Your name sounds on the coded voice of the bell.

I'll go nowhere you've not.
The bleached dip in a creature's bone's your throat.
That high lark, whatever it was you thought.

And this ridged stone your hand in mine,
and the curve of the turning earth your spine,
and the swooning bees besotted with flowers your tune.

I get up and walk. The dozing hillside is your dreaming head.
The cobblestones are every word you said.
The grave I kneel beside, only your bed.

Hour

Love's time's beggar, but even a single hour,
bright as a dropped coin, makes love rich.
We find an hour together, spend it not on flowers
or wine, but the whole of the summer sky and a grass ditch.

For thousands of seconds we kiss; your hair
like treasure on the ground; the Midas light
turning your limbs to gold. Time slows, for here
we are millionaires, backhanding the night

so nothing dark will end our shining hour,
no jewel hold a candle to the cuckoo spit
hung from the blade of grass at your ear,
no chandelier or spotlight see you better lit

than here. Now. Time hates love, wants love poor,
but love spins gold, gold, gold from straw.

Swing

Someone had looped a rope over a branch
and made a rough swing for the birch tree
next to the river. We passed it, walking and walking
into our new love; soft, unbearable dawns of desire
where mist was the water's slipping veil, or foam
boasted and frothed like champagne at the river's bend.

You asked me if I was sure, as a line of Canada geese
crowded the other bank, happy as wedding guests. Yes,
sure as the vision that flares in my head, away from you now,
of the moment you climbed on the swing, and swung out
into the silver air, the endless affirmative blue,
like something from heaven on earth, from paradise.

Rain

Not so hot as this for a hundred years.
You were where I was going. I was in tears.
I surrendered my heart to the judgement of my peers.

A century's heat in the garden, fierce as love.
You returned on the day that I had to leave.
I mimed the full, rich, busy life I had to live.

Hotter than hell. I burned for you day and night;
got bits of your body wrong, bits of it right,
in the huge mouth of the dark, in the bite of the light.

I planted a rose, burnt orange, the colour of flame,
gave it the last of the water, gave it your name.
It flared back at the sun in a perfect rhyme.

Then the rain came, like stammered kisses at first
on the back of my neck. I unfurled my fist
for the rain to caress with its lips. I turned up my face,

and water flooded my mouth, baptised my head,
and the rainclouds gathered like midnight overhead,
and the rain came down like a lover comes to a bed.

Absence

Then the birds stitching the dawn with their song
have patterned your name.

Then the green bowl of the garden filling with light
is your gaze.

Then the lawn lengthening and warming itself
is your skin.

Then a cloud disclosing itself overhead
is your opening hand.

Then the first seven bells from the church
pine on the air.

Then the sun's soft bite on my face
is your mouth.

Then a bee in a rose is your fingertip
touching me here.

Then the trees bending and meshing their leaves
are what we would do.

Then my steps to the river are text to a prayer
printing the ground.

Then the river searching its bank for your shape
is desire.

Then a fish nuzzling the water's throat
has a lover's ease.

Then a shawl of sunlight dropped in the grass
is a garment discarded.

Then a sudden scatter of summer rain
is your tongue.

Then a butterfly paused on a trembling leaf
is your breath.

Then the gauzy mist relaxed on the ground
is your pose.

Then the fruit from the cherry tree falling on grass
is your kiss, your kiss.

Then the day's hours are theatres of air
where I watch you entranced.

Then the sun's light going down from the sky
is the length of your back.

Then the evening bells over the rooftops
are lovers' vows.

Then the river staring up, lovesick for the moon,
is my long night.

Then the stars between us are love
urging its light.

If I Was Dead

If I was dead,
and my bones adrift
like dropped oars
in the deep, turning earth;

or drowned,
and my skull
a listening shell
on the dark ocean bed;

if I was dead,
and my heart
soft mulch
for a red, red rose;

or burned,
and my body
a fistful of grit, thrown
in the face of the wind;

if I was dead,
and my eyes,
blind at the roots of flowers,
wept into nothing,

I swear your love
would raise me
out of my grave,
in my flesh and blood,

like Lazarus;
hungry for this,
and this, and this,
your living kiss.

World

On the other side of the world,
you pass the moon to me,
like a loving cup,
or a quaich.
I roll you the sun.

I go to bed,
as you're getting up
on the other side of the world.
You have scattered the stars
towards me here, like seeds

in the earth.
All through the night,
I have sent you
bunches, bouquets, of cloud
to the other side of the world;

so my love will be shade
where you are,
and yours,
as I turn in my sleep,
the bud of a star.

Hand

Away from you, I hold hands with the air,
your imagined, untouchable hand. Not there,
your fingers braid with mine as I walk.
Far away in my heart, you start to talk.

I squeeze the air, kicking the auburn leaves,
everything suddenly gold. I half believe
your hand is holding mine, the way
it would if you were here. What do you say

in my heart? I bend my head to listen, then feel
your hand reach out and stroke my hair, as real
as the wind caressing the fretful trees above.
Now I can hear you clearly, speaking of love.

Rapture

Thought of by you all day, I think of you.
The birds sing in the shelter of a tree.
Above the prayer of rain, unacred blue,
not paradise, goes nowhere endlessly.
How does it happen that our lives can drift
far from our selves, while we stay trapped in time,
queuing for death? It seems nothing will shift
the pattern of our days, alter the rhyme
we make with loss to assonance with bliss.
Then love comes, like a sudden flight of birds
from earth to heaven after rain. Your kiss,
recalled, unstrings, like pearls, this chain of words.
Huge skies connect us, joining here to there.
Desire and passion on the thinking air.

Elegy

Who'll know then, when they walk by the grave
where your bones will be brittle things – this bone here
that swoops away from your throat, and this,
which perfectly fits the scoop of my palm, and these
which I count with my lips, and your skull,
which blooms on the pillow now, and your fingers,
beautiful in their little rings – that love, which wanders history,
singled you out in your time?

                        Love loved you best; lit you
with a flame, like talent, under your skin; let you
move through your days and nights, blessed in your flesh,
blood, hair, as though they were lovely garments
you wore to pleasure the air. Who'll guess, if they read
your stone, or press their thumbs to the scars
of your dates, that were I alive, I would lie on the grass
above your bones till I mirrored your pose, your infinite grace?

Row

But when we rowed,
the room swayed and sank down on its knees,
the air hurt and purpled like a bruise,
the sun banged the gate in the sky and fled.

But when we rowed,
the trees wept and threw away their leaves,
the day ripped the hours from our lives,
the sheets and pillows shredded themselves on the bed.

But when we rowed,
our mouths knew no kiss, no kiss, no kiss,
our hearts were jagged stones in our fists,
the garden sprouted bones, grown from the dead.

But when we rowed,
your face blanked like a page erased of words,
my hands squeezed themselves, burned like verbs,
love turned, and ran, and cowered in our heads.

Cuba

No getting up from the bed in this grand hotel
and getting dressed, like a work of art
rubbing itself out. No lifting the red rose
from the room service tray when you leave,
as though you might walk to the lip of a grave
and toss it down. No glass of champagne, left
to go flat in the glow of a bedside lamp,
the frantic bubbles swimming for the light. No white towel,
strewn, like a shroud, on the bathroom floor.
No brief steam on the mirror there for a finger
to smudge in a heart, an arrow, a name. No soft soap
rubbed between four hands. No flannel. No future plans.
No black cab, sad hearse, on the rank. No queue there.
No getting away from this. No goodnight kiss. No Cuba.

Tea

I like pouring your tea, lifting
the heavy pot, and tipping it up,
so the fragrant liquid steams in your china cup.

Or when you're away, or at work,
I like to think of your cupped hands as you sip,
as you sip, of the faint half-smile of your lips.

I like the questions – sugar? milk? –
and the answers I don't know by heart, yet,
for I see your soul in your eyes, and I forget.

Jasmine, Gunpowder, Assam, Earl Grey, Ceylon,
I love tea's names. Which tea would you like? I say,
but it's any tea, for you, please, any time of day,

as the women harvest the slopes,
for the sweetest leaves, on Mount Wu-Yi,
and I am your lover, smitten, straining your tea.

Betrothal

I will be yours, be yours.
I'll walk on the moors
with my spade.
Make me your bride.

I will be brave, be brave.
I'll dig my own grave
and lie down.
Make me your own.

I will be good, be good.
I'll sleep in my blankets of mud
till you kneel above.
Make me your love.

I'll stay forever, forever.
I'll wade in the river,
wearing my gown of stone.
Make me the one.

I will obey, obey.
I'll float far away,
gargling my vows.
Make me your spouse.

I will say yes, say yes.
I'll sprawl in my dress
on my watery bed.
Make me be wed.

I'll wear your ring, your ring.
I'll dance and I'll sing
in the flames.
Make me your name.

I'll feel desire, desire.
I'll bloom in the fire.
I'll blush like a baby.
Make me your lady.

I'll say I do, I do.
I'll be ash in a jar, for you
to scatter my life.
Make me your wife.

Bridgewater Hall

Again, the endless northern rain between us
like a veil. Tonight, I know exactly where you are,
which row, which seat. I stand at my back door.
The light pollution blindfolds every star.

I hold my hand out to the rain, simply to feel it, wet
and literal. It spills and tumbles in my palm,
a broken rosary. Devotion to you lets me see
the concert hall, lit up, the other side of town,

then see you leave there, one of hundreds in the dark,
your black umbrella raised. If rain were words, could talk,
somehow, against your skin, I'd say look up, let it utter
on your face. Now hear my love for you. Now walk.

The Lovers

Pity the lovers,
who climb to the high room,
where the bed,
and the gentle lamps wait,
and disembark from their lives.
The deep waves of the night
lap at the window.

Time slips away
like land from a ship.
The moon, their own death,
follows them, cold,
cold in their blankets.
Pity the lovers, homeless,
with no country to sail to.

Fall

Short days. The leaves are falling
to the deadline of the ground, gold

as the pages of myth. I feel the cold earth
fall away from the sun, the light's heart harden.

I fall too, as if from the glinting plane overhead,
backwards, through fierce blue, though I only lie

in your arms, on our coats, the last hour of autumn,
grasping a fistful of yellowing grass as you move in me,

fall and fall and fall towards you, your passionate gravity.

Ship

In the end,
it was nothing more
than the toy boat of a boy
on the local park's lake,
where I walked with you.

But I knelt down
to watch it arrive,
its white sail shy
with amber light,
the late sun
bronzing the wave
that lifted it up,

my ship coming in
with its cargo of joy.

Love

Love is talent, the world love's metaphor.
Aflame, October's leaves adore the wind,
its urgent breath, whirl to their own death.
Not here, you're everywhere.

                       The evening sky
worships the ground, bears down, the land
yearns back in darkening hills. The night
is empathy, stars in its eyes for tears. Not here,

you're where I stand, hearing the sea, crazy
for the shore, seeing the moon ache and fret
for the earth. When morning comes, the sun, ardent,
covers the trees in gold, you walk

                       towards me,
out of the season, out of the light love reasons.

Give

Give me, you said, on our very first night,
the forest. I rose from the bed and went out,
and when I returned, you listened, enthralled,
to the shadowy story I told.

Give me the river,
you asked the next night, then I'll love you forever.
I slipped from your arms and was gone,
and when I came back, you listened, at dawn,
to the glittering story I told.

Give me, you said, the gold
from the sun. A third time, I got up and dressed,
and when I came home, you sprawled on my breast
for the dazzling story I told.

Give me
the hedgerows, give me the fields.
I slid from the warmth of our sheets,
and when I returned, to kiss you from sleep,
you stirred at the story I told.

Give me the silvery cold
of the moon. I pulled on my boots and my coat,
but when I came back, moonlight on your throat
outshone the pale story I told.

                    Give me, you howled,
on our sixth night together, the wind in the trees.
You turned to the wall as I left,
and when I came home, I saw you were deaf
to the blustering story I told.

                    Give me the sky, all the space
it can hold. I left you, the last night we loved,
and when I returned, you were gone with the gold,
and the silver, the river, the forest, the fields,
and this is the story I've told.

Quickdraw

I wear the two, the mobile and the landline phones,
like guns, slung from the pockets on my hips. I'm all
alone. You ring, quickdraw, your voice a pellet
in my ear, and hear me groan.

                                    You've wounded me.
Next time, you speak after the tone. I twirl the phone,
then squeeze the trigger of my tongue, wide of the mark.
You choose your spot, then blast me

                                    through the heart.
And this is love, high noon, calamity, hard liquor
in the old Last Chance saloon. I show the mobile
to the Sheriff; in my boot, another one's

concealed. You text them both at once. I reel.
Down on my knees, I fumble for the phone,
read the silver bullets of your kiss. Take this . . .
and this . . . and this . . . and this . . . and this . . .

Finding the Words

I found the words at the back of a drawer,
wrapped in black cloth, like three rings
slipped from a dead woman's hand, cold,
dull gold. I had held them before,

                              years ago,
then put them away, forgetting whatever it was
I could use them to say. I touched the first to my lips,
the second, the third, like a sacrament,
like a pledge, like a kiss,

                  and my breath
warmed them, the words I needed to utter this, small words,
and few. I rubbed at them till they gleamed in my palm –
I love you, I love you, I love you –
as though they were new.

December

The year dwindles and glows
to December's red jewel,
my birth month.

The sky blushes,
and lays its cheek
on the sparkling fields.

Then dusk swaddles the cattle,
their silhouettes
simple as faith.

These nights are gifts,
our hands unwrapping the darkness
to see what we have.

The train rushes, ecstatic,
to where you are,
my bright star.

Grace

Then, like a sudden, easy birth, grace –
rendered as light to the softening earth,
the moon stepping slowly backwards
out of the morning sky, reward
for the dark hours we took to arrive and kneel
at the silver river's edge near the heron priest,
anointed, given – what we would wish ourselves.

New Year

I drop the dying year behind me like a shawl
and let it fall. The urgent fireworks fling themselves
against the night, flowers of desire, love's fervency.
Out of the space around me, standing here, I shape
your absent body against mine. You touch me as the giving air.

Most far, most near, your arms are darkness, holding me,
so I lean back, lip-read the heavens talking on in light,
syllabic stars. I see, at last, they pray at us. Your breath
is midnight's, living, on my skin, across the miles between us,
fields and motorways and towns, the million lit-up little homes.

This love we have, grief in reverse, full rhyme, wrong place,
wrong time, sweet work for hands, the heart's vocation, flares
to guide the new year in, the days and nights far out upon the sky's
dark sea. Your mouth is snow now on my lips, cool, intimate, first kiss,
a vow. Time falls and falls through endless space, to when we are.

Chinatown

Writing it, I see how much I love the sound.
Chinatown. Chinatown. Chinatown.
We went down, the day of the Year of the Monkey,
dim sum and dragons bound.

        Your fair head
was a pearl in the mouth of the crowd. The fireworks
were as loud as love, if love were allowed
a sound. Our wishing children pressed their incense
into a bowl of sand

        in Chinatown, the smoke drifting off
like question marks over their heads. If I had said
what I'd wished, if I had asked you to tell me the words,
shifting up from your heart

        for your lips to sift,
at least I'd have heard their sound uttered by you,
although then nothing we'd wished for in Chinatown,
Chinatown, Chinatown, would ever come true.

Wintering

All day, slow funerals have ploughed the rain.
We've done again
that trick we have of turning love to pain.

Grey fades to black. The stars begin their lies,
nothing to lose.
I wear a shroud of cold beneath my clothes.

Night clenches in its fist the moon, a stone.
I wish it thrown.
I clutch the small stiff body of my phone.

Dawn mocks me with a gibberish of birds.
I hear your words,
they play inside my head like broken chords.

*

The garden tenses, lies face down, bereaved,
has wept its leaves.
The Latin names of plants blur like belief.

I walk on ice, it grimaces, then breaks.
All my mistakes
are frozen in the tight lock of my face.

Bare trees hold out their arms, beseech, entreat,
cannot forget.
The clouds sag with the burden of their weight.

The wind screams at the house, bitter, betrayed.
The sky is flayed,
the moon a fingernail, bitten and frayed.

*

Another night, the smuggling in of snow.
You come and go,
your footprints like a love letter below.

Then something shifts, elsewhere and out of sight,
a hidden freight
that morning brings in on a tide of light.

The soil grows hesitant, it blurts in green,
so what has been
translates to what will be, certain, unseen,

as pain turns back again to love, like this,
your flower kiss,
and winter thaws and melts, cannot resist.

Spring

Spring's pardon comes, a sweetening of the air,
the light made fairer by an hour, time
as forgiveness, granted in the murmured colouring
of flowers, rain's mantra of reprieve, reprieve, reprieve.

The lovers waking in the lightening rooms believe
that something holds them, as they hold themselves,
within a kind of grace, a soft embrace, an absolution
from their stolen hours, their necessary lies. And this is wise:

to know that music's gold is carried in the frayed purse
of a bird, to pick affection's herb, to see the sun and moon
half-rhyme their light across the vacant, papery sky.
Trees, in their blossoms, young queens, flounce for clemency.

Answer

If you were made of stone,
your kiss a fossil sealed up in your lips,
your eyes a sightless marble to my touch,
your grey hands pooling raindrops for the birds,
your long legs cold as rivers locked in ice,
if you were stone, if you were made of stone, yes, yes.

If you were made of fire,
your head a wild Medusa hissing flame,
your tongue a red-hot poker in your throat,
your heart a small coal glowing in your chest,
your fingers burning pungent brands on flesh,
if you were fire, if you were made of fire, yes, yes.

If you were made of water,
your voice a roaring, foaming waterfall,
your arms a whirlpool spinning me around,
your breast a deep, dark lake nursing the drowned,
your mouth an ocean, waves torn from your breath,
if you were water, if you were made of water, yes, yes.

If you were made of air,
your face empty and infinite as sky,
your words a wind with litter for its nouns,
your movements sudden gusts among the clouds,
your body only breeze against my dress,
if you were air, if you were made of air, yes, yes.

If you were made of air, if you were air,
if you were made of water, if you were water,
if you were made of fire, if you were fire,

if you were made of stone, if you were stone,
or if you were none of these, but really death,
the answer is yes, yes.

Treasure

A soft ounce of your breath
in my cupped palm.
The gold weight of your head
on my numb arm.

Your heart's warm ruby
set in your breast.
The art of your hands,
the slim turquoise veins under your wrists.

Your mouth, the sweet, chrism blessing
of its kiss,
the full measure of bliss pressed
to my lips.

Your fine hair, run through my fingers,
sieved.
Your silver smile, your jackpot laugh,
bright gifts.

Sighted amber, the 1001 nights
of your eyes.
Even the sparkling fool's gold
of your lies.

Presents

I snipped and stitched my soul
to a little black dress,

hung my heart on a necklace,
tears for its pearls,

my mouth went for a bracelet,
gracing your arm,

all my lover's words
for its dangling charms,

and my mind was a new hat,
sexy and chic,

for a hair of your head on my sleeve
like a scrawled receipt.

Write

Write that the sun bore down on me,
kissing and kissing, and my face
reddened, blackened, whitened to ash,
was blown away by the passionate wind
over the fields, where my body's shape
still flattened the grass, to end as dust
in the eyes of my own ghost.

                        Or write
that the river held me close in its arms, cold fingers
stroking my limbs, cool tongue probing my mouth,
water's voice swearing its love love love in my ears,
as I drowned in belief.

                    Then write the moon
striding down from the sky in its silver boots
to kick me alive; the stars like a mob of light,
chanting a name, yours. Write your name on my lips
when I entered the dark church of the wood
like a bride, lay down for my honeymoon,
and write the night, sexy as hell, write the night
pressing and pressing my bones
into the ground.

Venus

(6.19 a.m., 8th June 2004)

The jet of your pupil
set in the gold of your eye –

nor can I see

the dark fruit of your nipple
ripe on your breast –

nor can I feel

the tip of my tongue
burn in the star of your mouth –

nor can I hold

the small pulse at your wrist
under my thumb –

but I can watch

the transit of Venus
over the face of the sun.

Whatever

I'll take your hand, the left,
and ask that it still have life
to hold my hand, the right,
as I walk alone where we walked,
or to lie all night on my breast,
at rest, or to stop all talk with a finger
pressed to my lips.

                I'll take your lips,
ask, when I close my eyes, as though
in prayer, that they ripen out of the air
to be there again on mine,
or to say my name, or to smile, or to kiss
the sleep from my eyes. I'll take

                          your eyes,
nothing like, lovelier under, the sun,
and ask that they wake to see, to look
at me, even to cry, so long as I feel their tears
on your face, warm rain on a rose.

Your face I'll take, asleep, ask that I learn,
by heart, the tilt of your nose; or awake, and ask
that I touch with my tongue the soft buds of the lobes
of your ears

            and I'll take them, too,
ask that they feel my breath shape
into living words, that they hear.

I'll take your breath
and ask that it comes and goes, comes and goes, forever,

like the blush under your cheek, and I'll even settle for that. Whatever.

Midsummer Night

Not there to see midsummer's midnight rose
open and bloom, me,
or there when the river dressed in turquoise
under the moon, you;
not there when stones softened, opened, showed
the fossils they held
or there, us, when the dark sky fell to the earth
to gather its smell.

Not there when a strange bird sang on a branch
over our heads, you
and me, or there when a starlit fruit ripened
itself on a tree.
Not there to lie on the grass of our graves, both,
alive alive oh,
or there for Shakespeare's shooting star,
or for who we are,

but elsewhere, far. Not there for the magic hour
when time becomes love
or there for light's pale hand to slip, slender,
from darkness's glove.
Not there when our young ghosts called to us
from the other side
or there where the heron's rags were a silver gown,
by grace of the light.

Not there to be right, to find our souls, we,
dropped silks on the ground,
or there to be found again by ourselves, you, me,
mirrored in water.

Not there to see constellations spell themselves on the sky
and black rhyme with white
or there to see petals fold on a rose like a kiss
on midsummer night.

Grief

Grief, your gift, unwrapped,
my empty hands made heavy,
holding when they held you
like an ache; unlooked for,
though my eyes stare inward now
at where you were, my star, my star;
and undeserved, the perfect choice
for one with everything, humbling
my heart; unwanted, too, my small voice
lost for words to thank you with; unusual,
how it, given, grows to fill a day, a night,
a week, a month, teaching its text,
love's spinster twin, my head bowed,
learning, learning; understood.

Ithaca

And when I returned,
I pulled off my stiff and salty sailor's clothes,
slipped on the dress of the girl I was,
and slid overboard.
A mile from Ithaca, I anchored the boat.

The evening softened and spread,
the turquoise water mentioning its silver fish,
the sky stooping to hear.
My hands moved in the water, moved on the air,
the lover I was, tracing your skin, your hair,

and Ithaca there, the bronze mountains
shouldered like rough shields,
the caves, where dolphins hid,
dark pouches for jewels,
the olive trees ripening their tears in our pale fields.

Then I drifted in on a ribbon of light,
tracking the scents of rosemary, lemon, thyme,
the fragrances of your name,
which I chanted again in my heart,
like the charm it was, bringing me back

to Ithaca, all hurt zeroed now
by the harm you could do with a word,
me as hero plainly absurd,
wading in, waist-high, from the shallows at dusk,
dragging my small white boat.

Land

If we were shades
who walked here once
over the heather, over the shining stones,
fresh in our skin and bones
with all of the time to come
left to be us,

if we were dust,
once flesh, where a cloud
swoons on the breast of a hill,
breathing here still
in our countable days,
the words we said,

snagged on the air
like the murmuring bees,
as we lay by the loch,
parting our clothes with our hands
to feel who we were,
we would rather be there

than where we are here,
all that was due to us
still up ahead,
if we were shades or dust
who lived love
before we were long dead.

Night Marriage

When I turn off the light
and the dark mile between us
crumples and falls,
you slip from your self
to wait for me in my sleep,
the face of the moon sinking into a cloud;

or I wake bereaved
from the long hours
I spend in your dreams,
an owl in the forest crying its soft vowels,
dark fish swimming under the river's skin.

Night marriage. The small hours join us,
face to face as we sleep and dream;
the whole of the huge night is our room.

Syntax

I want to call you thou, the sound
of the shape of the start
of a kiss – like this, thou –
and to say, after, I love,
thou, I love, thou I love, not
I love you.

       Because I so do –
as we say now – I want to say
thee, I adore, I adore thee,
and to know in my lips
the syntax of love resides,
and to gaze in thine eyes.

Love's language starts, stops, starts;
the right words flowing or clotting in the heart.

Snow

You come back,
after my three-month night,
as I knew you would, like light, light.
And though it is summer's height,
sexy with thunder, rainy heat,
you talk of snow.

                  It is gathering now,
packing the freight of itself
into cold, faraway clouds,
miles out at sea,
crying upwards into the black sky;

each flake unique, that will fall on us, as we kiss,
or I tell you the poem by Louis MacNeice.
The room was suddenly rich . . .

Your Move

Now you've moved
to my neck of the woods,
let me show you around.

The name scarred
on all of the trees
is your own.

The blood poised,
red rain on the thorn
of a rose, mine.

The goblin, crouched
under that dripping bush,
your servant, ma'am.

The lightning,
frantic to touch,
means you no harm.

The thunder,
tendering huge words,
is spelling a charm.

The local news
starting as prose
ends in a rhyme.

The inns and taverns
are dusting off
their finest of wines,

and the air we breathe,
I say to myself,
is the same, the same.

Epiphany

Not close my eyes to the light
when the light
is in my head,
        or sleep
when only your, only thy warm skin
is my bed,
        or live, when days, nights,
sightless of you, sightless of thee,
are hours with the dead,
           or talk sense
when words, when words,
are the cauls of the unsaid,
          or believe when belief
is a light gone out yet burning, gold, red.

The Love Poem

Till love exhausts itself, longs
for the sleep of words –
                              my mistress' eyes –
to lie on a white sheet, at rest
in the language –
                        let me count the ways –
or shrink to a phrase like an epitaph –
                                            come live
with me –
or fall from its own high cloud as syllables
in a pool of verse –
                        one hour with thee.

Till love gives in and speaks
in the whisper of art –
                              dear heart,
how like you this? –
love's lips pursed to quotation marks
kissing a line –
                        look in thy heart
and write –
love's light fading, darkening,
black as ink on a page –
                              there is a garden
in her face.

Till love is all in the mind –

                    O my America!

my new-found land –
or all in the pen
in the writer's hand –

                    behold, thou art fair –

not there, except in a poem,
known by heart like a prayer,
both near and far,
near and far –

                    the desire of the moth

for the star.

Art

Only art now – our bodies, brushstroke, pigment, motif;
our story, figment, suspension of disbelief;
the thrum of our blood, percussion;
chords, minor, for the music of our grief.

Art, the chiselled, chilling marble of our kiss;
locked into soundless stone, our promises,
or fizzled into poems; page print
for the dried flowers of our voice.

No choice for love but art's long illness, death,
huge theatres for the echoes that we left,
applause, then utter dark;
grand opera for the passion of our breath;

and the Oscar-winning movie in your heart;
and where my soul sang, croaking art.

Unloving

Learn from the winter trees, the way
they kiss and throw away their leaves,
then hold their stricken faces in their hands
and turn to ice;

        or from the clocks,
looking away, unloving light, the short days
running out of things to say; a church
a ghost ship on a sea of dusk.

Learn from a stone, its heart-shape meaningless,
perfect with relentless cold; or from the bigger moon,
implacably dissolving in the sky, or from the stars,
lifeless as Latin verbs.

        Learn from the river,
flowing always somewhere else, even its name,
change, change; learn from a rope
hung from a branch like a noose, a crow cursing,

a dead heron mourned by a congregation of flies.
Learn from the dumbstruck garden, summer's grave,
where nothing grows, not a Beast's rose;
from the torn veil of a web;

        from our daily bread:
perpetual rain, nothing like tears, unloving clouds;
language unloving love; even this stale air
unloving all the spaces where you were.

Over

'That's the wise thrush; he sings each song twice over,
Lest you should think he never could recapture
The first fine careless rapture!'

ROBERT BROWNING

I wake to a dark hour out of time, go to the window.
No stars in this black sky, no moon to speak of, no name
or number to the hour, no skelf of light. I let in air.
The garden's sudden scent's an open grave.
What do I have

            to help me, without spell or prayer,
endure this hour, endless, heartless, anonymous,
the death of love? Only the other hours –
the air made famous where you stood,
the grand hotel, flushing with light, which blazed us
on the night,

            the hour it took for you
to make a ring of grass and marry me. I say your name
again. It is a key, unlocking all the dark,
so death swings open on its hinge.
I hear a bird begin its song,
piercing the hour, to bring first light this Christmas dawn,
a gift, the blush of memory.

62